GLASGOW
Colouring Book

Illustrated by John MacGregor

First published by HOMETOWN WORLD in 2011
Hometown World Ltd, 7 Northumberland Buildings, Bath BA1 2JB
www.hometownworld.co.uk
Copyright © Hometown World Ltd 2011

ISBN 978-1-84993-196-0
Printed in China

CHILDHOOD DREAMS
HOMETOWN WORLD

Colourful Clyde

Draw over the dotted lines to finish the Tall Ship Glenlee. Then colour it in.

Fun Fact
The Glenlee was launched in Glasgow in 1896 and sailed four times around the world!

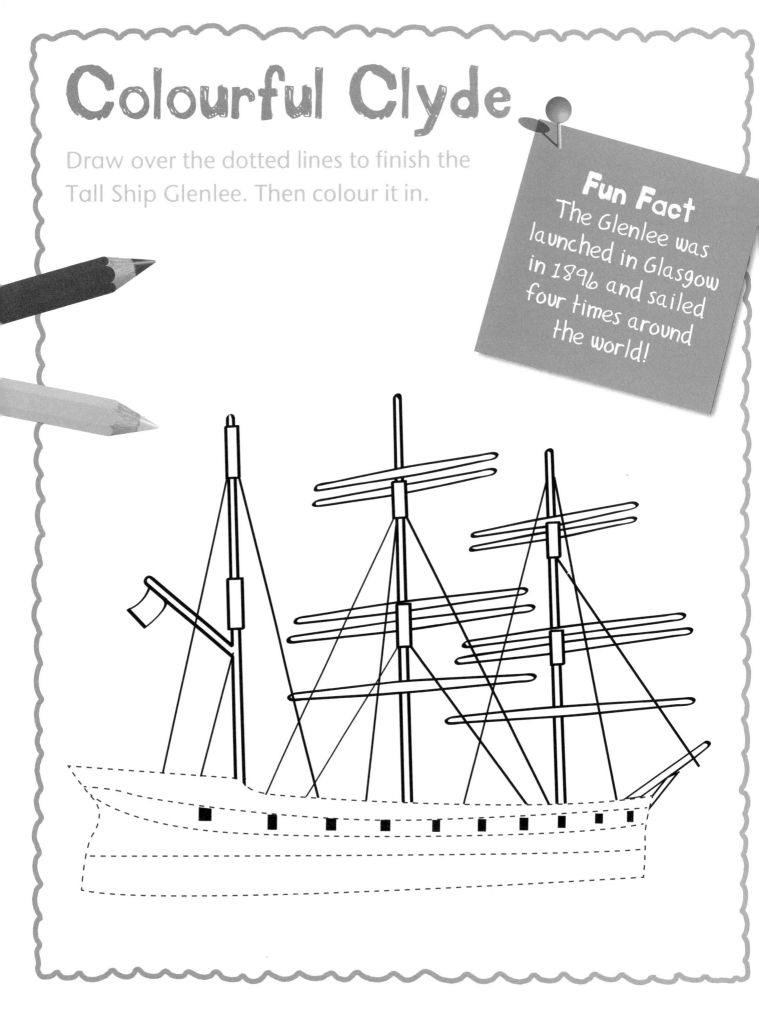

Try!

Draw over the dotted lines
to finish the Scottish flag.
Then colour it blue and white.

Fun Fact
There has been
a Glasgow rugby
team since 1872.

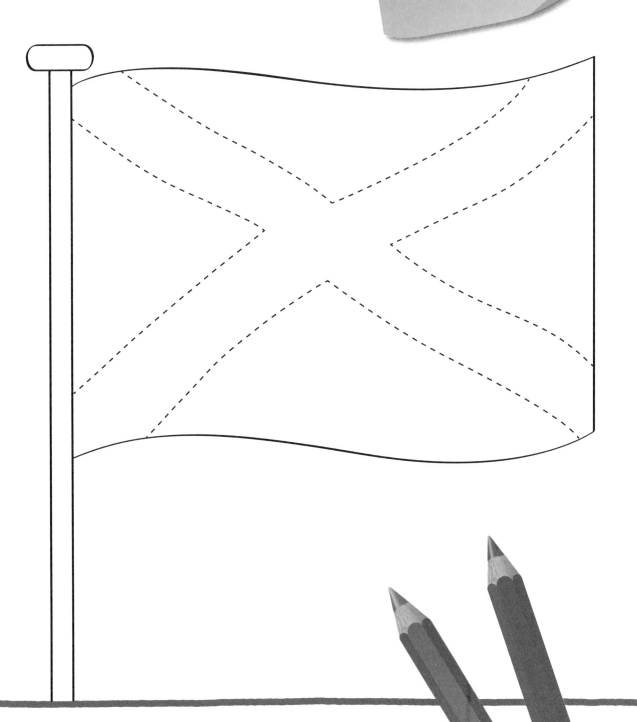

Alexandra Park

Add a golf ball near the hole to win the game. Then colour in the picture.

Fun Fact
Alexandra Park is named after Princess Alexandra who opened it in 1870.

Let's Go!

Draw over the dotted lines to finish the trolleybus. Then colour it in.

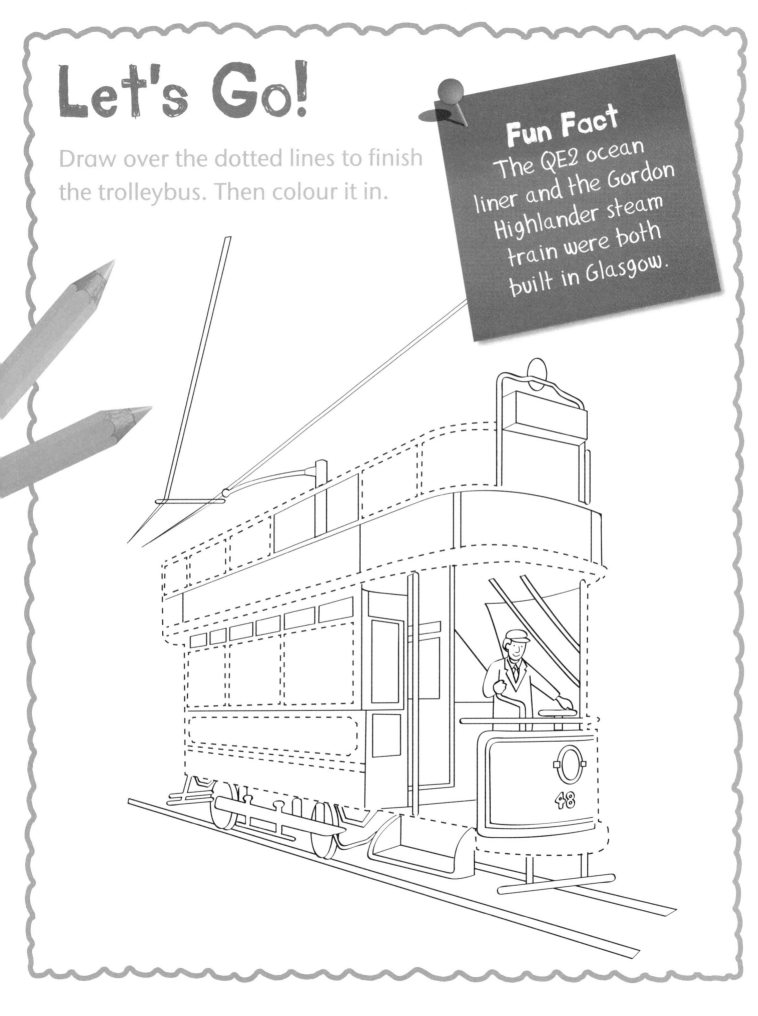

Go Glasgow!

Draw two ski poles.
Then colour in the skier.

Change at Glasgow

Choose the letters to finish the place names. Then colour in the picture.

B L S D Y S R G

Departures

Edin_urgh	14.09
East Ki_bride	14.26
Neil_ton	14.44
Lon_on Euston	
A_r	
Pai_ley Canal	
Kilma_nock	
Lar_s	

Fun Fact
The first TV pictures sent by John Logie Baird were between London and Central Hotel Glasgow in 1927.

Seeing the Sights

Draw over the dotted lines to finish the bus. Add two people on the bus, then colour it in.

BUS STOP

Picnic in the Park

Draw your favourite picnic food on the plate. Then colour it in.

Fun Fact
Some of the tree ferns growing in Kibble Palace glasshouse are over 100 years old!

Waterfront

Add a hook and chain to the end of the crane like it had when it was first built. Then colour it in.

Goal!

Colour in your team's football strip and add a number.

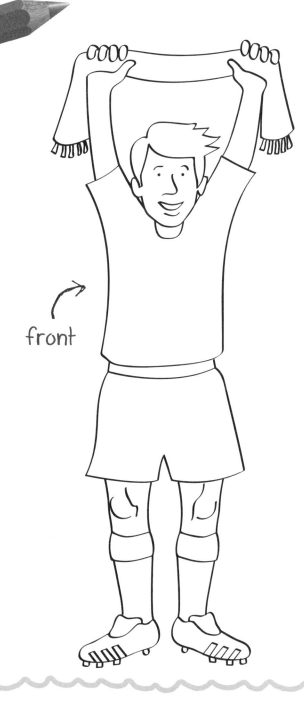

front

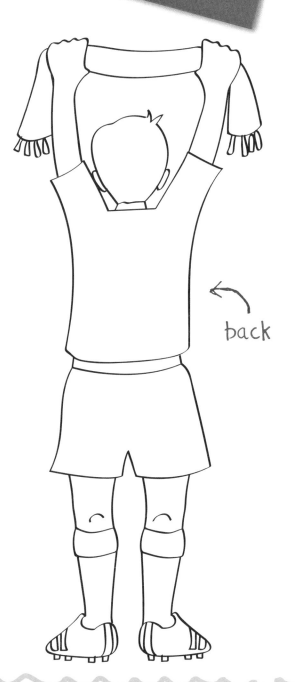

back

Flying High

Draw a colourful pattern on the kite. Add bows to the tail.

Thrills and Spills

Add horns to the highland cattle.
Then colour in the picture.

Picture Perfect

Draw a picture of yourself.
Then decorate the picture frame.

Fun on the Green

Draw over the dotted lines to finish the Scottish piper's hat and bagpipes. Then colour him in.

Fun Fact
World Pipe Band Championships are held on Glasgow Green every August.

Fun at the Fair

Add poles to join the horses on the merry-go-round. Then colour it in.

Whizz Bang!

Colour in the fireworks!

Fun Fact
The Chinese were making fireworks over 2,000 years ago.

Braw!

Wow!

Colourful fireworks light up the sky for Hogmanay!